Belinda Jane Robinson

Beli... ...an ...ex ...which she sold in London and New York. After she married she trained as a reflexologist and started a company (www.relaxology.com) offering 'chill out' areas at Exhibitions and Corporate Events in the UK and Europe.

Born and brought up in the Far East, she spent many years of her life going between the East and the West. Her Eastern roots had more influences on her than she ever thought possible and over the past few years she has been on an incredible journey of self-discovery.

Driven by a passion to encourage girls and women in particular to value and empower themselves, Belinda suggests a formula using seven jewels to represent seven areas of our lives to focus upon in order to lay down a foundation for a rich and fulfilling life.

Disclaimer — the contents of this book are purely as a result of the author's own personal life experiences and are her interpretations as to how this helped her. It is in no way intended to be a substitute for professional consultations.

www.sevenjewelsoflife.com

Preface

I wrote this little book on the Lizard peninsular in Cornwall with its magical coastline and the hypnotic Helford River. The incredible wild beauty of this area offered me a place to regenerate and soothe my soul.

The purpose of this book is to take you on a journey — not just an ordinary journey — this is a journey back to a place that you have perhaps forgotten about — or you didn't even know was there... This is a journey back to your heart. Life is a journey with ups and downs and twists and turns and it's so easy to get lost along the way — forget where you are going and why... but... wouldn't it be amazing if you had the knowledge to get yourself back on track... to connect and stay connected to your true source of peace and happiness?

I am going to share with you a little of my journey — which has taken me on some ups and downs and which in the end finally led me to write The Seven Jewels of Life.

Acknowlededgments

With special love and thanks to Lucy and Jenny my two wonderful daughters who were my inspiration, Jane and Robbie my parents, Charlie Robinson my amazing brother and wise counsellor, Annie my lovely sister, Connie my first best friend and lifelong rock, Diana my first Diamond Sister and gentle anchor in Cornwall at Cornubia, Sue L, Roseanne, Carey, Alison C, Maria, Lorraine, Corinne, Ginny, Alison S, Caroline C, Deborah, Maggie Lake, Stan. All my Diamond Sisters, you know who you are... The men I have loved and who have loved me, my friends and family past, present and future, Brandon for his endless patience working on this book, RB for offering such great support and encouragement, Rishi, Kelvin Heard — healer and friend and link to Rishi, Mother Meera, Deepak Chopra, Louise Hay, Bob Proctor, Wayne Dyer, Byron Katie, Eckhart Tolle, Bob Dylan, Joni Mitchell, Katherine Woodward Thomas, Claire Zammit, Jean Houston, Jane Goodall, Malala. The beauty and spirit of Cornwall, the magical Trelowarren estate, the Polpeor Café on Lizard Point where I would go to write gazing across the sea, England, the amazingness of India, The Malay Archipelago, this incredible planet and everyone and everything in it, Mozart, the poet Rumi, the poets of England, Shakespeare, George my Golden Labrador companion in Cornwall, tigers, and my cat Charlie...

❀ ❀ ❀

Contents

❀ ❀ ❀

PART 1

My Treasure Box of Jewels

I was born in Singapore, though brought up on rubber plantations in Malaya (now Malaysia) by my mother Jane and my father Robbie — along with my older sister Annie and younger brother Charlie. My father lived and worked in Malaya for 45 years. He was captured at the fall of Singapore in 1942 and spent the war as a Prisoner of War on the Thai-Burma railway before returning to manage rubber plantations once more. The East has always stayed deep in my psyche and soul and has had more influences on me than I ever realised or thought possible.

I loved my home in Malaya — the blue skies, the humid days, the crashing afternoon thunderstorms, sitting beneath the jacaranda tree, the bright green paddy fields, warm smiling faces, the dense jungle, the temple bells... the cock crowing at dawn and the freedom to run barefoot and wild.

At seven years old I was sent off to boarding school in England. I remember a great sense of excitement as the whole family packed up our belongings on the plantation and made our way down to Singapore docks to start the sea voyage to England. It was to be a magical journey... our first stop — elephant rides in Colombo — then on to Bombay (now Mumbai) to experience the amazingness of India for the first time. Onwards we sailed across the Arabian Sea listening to tales of Sinbad the Sailor, then gliding up the Suez Canal haggling with the gully-gully men as we heard the calls to prayer across the desert sands. We entered the Mediterranean Sea at Port Said and made our way past the Rock of Gibraltar to Tilbury docks, London, England. Overnight I felt as if I had landed on an alien planet.

❀ ❀ ❀

Once in England, preparations began in earnest for boarding school and before I knew it I was saying tearful farewells to my parents.

As the school door went bang... my heart went BANG...

I felt numb with fear... unable to speak up for myself — and no one was listening anyway...

Looking back — what gave me a form of escapism and moments of great joy and peace during those difficult early days at school were two gifts I cherished.

The first was a small globe my father gave me so that I could look at home — Malaya — on the map and remember our sea voyage and all the places we had seen together — I called this globe 'my world'.

The other was a gift my mother had given me. It was a small treasure box. It came from a side street vendor in Singapore and in it I kept seven brightly coloured make-believe jewels made of glass or paste, and wrapped up in a small piece of golden cloth was my prize jewel... a glittering glass diamond.

Every night in our dormitories we were allowed some quiet time before 'lights out'. It was the best time of the day for me. I would place 'my world' on my bed and then open the lid of my treasure box and look at all my beautiful jewels, polishing each one in turn to prevent homesickness from taking hold. As I was polishing my jewels I would start to imagine myself having wonderful and exciting adventures.

Flying on a magic carpet across the Arabian Peninsula — riding on a tiger's back in Rajasthan — as a slave girl on the banks of the River Nile rescued by a handsome prince — sailing the seven seas in a boat with billowing sails — but in all my adventures I would always be wearing my jewels...

When it was time for 'lights out' in my dormitory I would carefully place all the jewels back in the treasure box and as a last treat I would dive under the covers with my torch and holding my wonderful diamond up to the light — seeing that it reflected all the colours of each of the other jewels — all the colours of the rainbow... I would make a wish... and drift off to sleep... to dream.

After leaving school I spent a few months exploring Malaysia, the beautiful country I called home, before running off to live in Switzerland with my first love... I then worked as a fashion model in Europe — eventually returning to London to train as a nurse at the Middlesex Hospital.

On my days off from nursing, my imagination and creativity started to tug at me and quite spontaneously I started to design a range of clothing which I sold at the Covent Garden Market. A year later I made the decision to open a tiny shop called 'Belinda Jane' and I started to supply Harrods, Liberty's and Bergdorf Goodman in New York. After I married I put 'Belinda Jane' on hold to concentrate on my family — and trained as a reflexologist.

Then a few years ago, I hit a particularly difficult time in my personal life as my 25-year marriage sadly fell apart... it felt as though my whole word was collapsing around me — as can often happen to us all in our lives in one way or another. Emotional pain is so underrated — no one can see a physical scar on the outside... but the pain is just as great, if not greater.

3   ✿ ✿ ✿

I felt numb... it took me right back to those early school days when the door went bang and my heart went BANG... I felt disconnected and desperate and on the wrong path... and wondering: how do I move forward again?

I found myself thinking a lot about my mother who died at just 59 years old and wishing she was here to advise and guide me. One afternoon as I was in the attic clearing out I came across a wooden crate. It was full of old letters, photos and knick-knacks and then I saw it — the gift that my mother had given me 50 years ago... my best friend — my treasure box of jewels.

I opened the lid to see all the jewels still there after all those years... lifting my heart as they always did and there, wrapped up in a small piece of golden cloth, was my prize jewel, my diamond.

I took the treasure box downstairs to my desk and felt drawn to pick up the ruby... I started to polish it just as I used to... but this time I found myself thinking about my life purpose and sensed that something inside me was stirring ...

I picked up my pen and started to write about what I thought my life purpose might be... words just seemed to pour out onto the pages. I started to disconnect from my sadness, daring to imagine that there may be another story... a beautiful story — and that perhaps the sad and disempowered person I had become wasn't the me I was born to be... that I had a unique contribution to make... a life purpose to discover...

Every day I would look forward to connecting with this peaceful space — I call it 'The Diamond Field' — and to picking out another jewel to see what I was inspired to write about. I found that each of the Seven Jewels led me to consider a different facet of my life that I needed to get into balance with and pay attention to as a way of getting back onto the right path.

❀ ❀ ❀

As I started to incorporate what I had written relating to the Seven Jewels into my daily life, a peaceful space opened up within me offering light in my darkness and I felt a huge sense of relief which I had not felt for such a long time.

Having two daughters now in their 20s, their friends were often going through their own life challenges including heart breaks and breakups — even with beauty and youth on their side they still had a sense that they weren't enough... I came to see that many people know intuitively that something is missing and that perhaps we haven't been taught something that is key... that somehow we are not privy to our self-worth, which can make all the difference...

I started to share how the jewels were helping me with these young women as well as with my reflexology clients and I found that they seemed to like it and find it helpful. Through their positive feedback I began to sense that not only could I use this formula to turn myself around — but that I could help others do the same.

People have been talking about ways to find inner peace and happiness for centuries, and we are particularly lucky to be living at a time when there are so many great teachers available to help and guide us at this confusing time of great change on our planet. Over the years I have read several of their works and listened to many hours of their wisdom, which has always inspired and lifted me and for which I am eternally grateful.

One day I received a call from Diana — my dear friend in Cornwall — we had trained as nurses together all those years ago and although I had not told her what I was going through, she must have picked up on it — she kindly invited me to come and stay with her in Cornwall. I packed a few things including my copious notes on The Seven Jewels — went for a week and eventually stayed for two years... Diana's husband was suffering with serious health issues and as he eventually became terminally ill we found that our unconditional friendship — helping each other as best we could — was a blessing, as it supported us beautifully as we tried to navigate ourselves through this traumatic period in both our lives.

Walking along the 'Serpentine Stone' cliff paths of the Lizard peninsula was just the gentle energy needed and I would often go to ponder and write at the Polpeor Café at Lizard Point — the most southerly point of England. Gazing out to sea I imagined the whole world spreading down before me, around me and above me — the great oceans and continents full of life. In the distance I could see Lizard Point lighthouse standing in a field of beautiful wild flowers — its comforting beacon of diamond light gently rotating and reflecting all the colours of the rainbow, offering refuge and hope to many in the storms...

I felt so grateful for this opportunity to spend time in the beauty of nature which allowed me the mental space to process my notes and to start to transform my pain into something positive — into this book to help others — The Seven Jewels of Life.

It dawned on me that perhaps I had found my life purpose.

Lizard Lighthouse — Cornwall   2012

❀ ❀ ❀   6

Your Treasure Box of Jewels

Each one of you has a 'Treasure Box of Jewels' with your own unique 'Diamond' hiding deep within you, and your lives are actually about being on an incredible treasure hunt to rediscover these jewels.

Each jewel represents an area of your life and it's up to you to find them and listen to the messages that each one has for you. Your jewels offer you a road map to keep you on track, guiding you towards your unique destiny.

Often we find one or two of the jewels and concentrate on them, forgetting about the others, and then wonder why it feels as if something is missing in your life.

Let's go on a treasure hunt to find all your jewels...

After you have read this book through you will find there is Dream Sheet for you to complete in your own time — giving you an opportunity to consider what each Jewel represents to you.

The Jewels

Each Jewel represents an area of our lives for us to focus on.

- A jewel of the day
- A colour of the day — if possible, wear an item of this colour on that day
- An emotion to work on
- An affirmation to speak
- Actions to take

Focus on the World

Each day there is a continent of the world to focus on encouraging us to celebrate their music, culture, food and wisdom.

Ever since I was given my small globe that I called 'my world', I have always loved looking at globes and maps and finding out where we all come from, and been fascinated by this amazing planet.

It is through celebrating our differences that we can start to break down barriers, building respect for each other — and, in these times of great change on the planet, sow the seeds of hope and tolerance in our lives to unite us.

A little bit more about the Jewels and their meanings...

I am often asked why I chose a certain jewel to represent the various areas of life or why I chose to celebrate a particular continent on a particular day — all I can say is that this is just how it happened for me — I noted the jewel I had spontaneously taken out of the treasure box, the day of the week I had picked it and what that jewel represented to me... it just unfolded naturally that way. This was the same for the emotions, and the affirmations I chose.

Ruby

Represents: Life purpose
Also represents: Education, work, finances

Day of the week: Monday

Colour: Red

Emotion: Self-worth, self-esteem, courage, confidence

Affirmation: My self-esteem is growing stronger every day.
I am responsible for discovering my true life purpose.

Focus on the World: Africa — Celebrate their music, culture, food and wisdom

Quotes: "I learned that courage was not the absence of fear, but the triumph over it. The brave man is not he who does not feel afraid but he who conquers that fear."
Nelson Mandela

"The one who asks questions doesn't lose his way."
African Proverb

9 ❊ ❊ ❊

The Ruby represents Life Purpose

We are all put onto this planet for a reason and it's up to you and nobody else to find out who you are and why you are here... what you were born to do.

There is at least one thing you can do which is better than anyone on the planet. What are your unique talents, and how can you best serve humanity and others using these gifts in your work? Education is key; study hard, work hard, the prize is immense, it opens up the door to freedom...

Where is Your Ruby hiding? How will you know when you find your purpose? Throughout your life you are given clues as to where your ruby may be hiding by how it makes you feel... Where is it leading you to express yourself? What do you want to do? What makes you feel alive and fulfilled? What do you feel drawn to do?

Action: Imagine that you are already doing what you want and then start to plan some actions towards your goals... perhaps work as a volunteer or arrange some work experience in that area, and put some time aside to study more about the subject. It's easy to have theories about what you may or may not like but you will never know until you have tried it for a while.

Also today: Read books that interest and inspire you — study something just for fun... check out your finances. Create a daily routine to give structure to your day.

How will you know when you have found your Ruby?
By how it makes you feel when you are living your life purpose and laying down a strong foundation for a rich, joyful and fulfilling life celebrating your uniqueness. This will then develop a sense of self-worth and self-esteem which is priceless and which ultimately leaves a unique legacy of contribution behind you.

❀ ❀ ❀

Topaz

Represents: Creativity
Also represents: Hobbies, travel and transport, dreams.

Day of the week: Tuesday

Colour: Orange

Emotion: Self-expression, imagination, creativity, transformation

Affirmation: I imagine my dreams already manifested
I am free to express the uniqueness of who I truly am in all areas of my life

Focus on the World: Australasia and New Zealand — Celebrate their music, culture, food and wisdom

Quotes: "We are all visitors to this time, this place. We are just passing through. Our purpose here is to observe, to learn, to grow, to love... and then we return Home."
Australian Aboriginal Wisdom

"Turn your face to the sun and the shadows fall behind you."
"Never spend time with those who do not respect you."
Maori Wisdom

❀ ❀ ❀

The Topaz represents Creativity

Your imagination is the key that unlocks the door to your creativity. Everything creative starts as a thought in our imagination — look around you — the chair you are sitting on — the pictures on the walls, the pen you are writing with all started as a seed in someone's imagination... so dare to imagine... dare to dream...

"Those who lose dreaming are lost." Aboriginal Proverb.

Where is Your Topaz hiding? What clues is it leaving for you?

Where is it leading you to express yourself to contact your own uniqueness — is it through music, singing, dance, drama, the arts, writing, enjoying a creative hobby... You can be creative in the way you dress and cook — in the way you decorate your home... you can be creative at work... in the way you live... everywhere...

 Action: Create your own Dream Sheet today. You could make a copy and look at it during the day, imagining all your dreams are on their way as you prepare to take whatever action is needed towards their fulfilment.

Also today: Let yourself go and dance to your favourite music for five minutes... smile and feel the life force pulsing through your veins... get in touch with your uniqueness and celebrate it... if you can plan a holiday or a short trip away or take a day off to explore somewhere new, pay attention to any mode of transport you may have — check your tyre pressures, clean your bike, arrange to go to a concert or visit an art gallery or start a creative project.

How will you know when you have found your Topaz? Because as you start to celebrate your uniqueness you will discover you have an essential and unique contribution to make to the future of our world... it will all start to make sense... your Topaz will open the door for you...

❀ ❀ ❀

Citrine

Represents: Charity
Also represents: Computers and technology, humour

Day of the Week: Wednesday

Colour: Yellow

Emotion: Confidence, courage, humour, generosity and humility

Affirmation: I live my life with confidence and courage. I love to laugh. I am making a difference to the world with my unique gifts

Focus on the World: The Middle East — Celebrate their music, culture, food and wisdom

Quotes: "Let yourself be drawn by the stronger pull of that which you truly love."
Rumi — 13th century mystic poet

"Do not be wise in words — be wise in deeds."
Jewish proverb

The Citrine represents Charity

One of our basic human needs is to contribute and make a difference. We all lead such hectic lives that this often seems an intrusion, but the rewards to reaching out to others are immense.

Where is your Citrine hiding? What clues is it leaving for you? How can you serve and make a difference in your community... your country — our world... it's all about making a difference.

Action: Brighten up someone's day today with a smile, a compliment, carrying a bag, opening a door... think about doing some voluntary work, or if you have a little spare time perhaps call up your local old peoples' home and ask to visit someone who never has visitors.

We are essentially social beings and these simple interactions with other human beings — making a difference to their lives without wanting anything in return is so powerful and so rewarding.

Also today: Brush up on computer and technical knowledge and remember to laugh and smile — humour and laughter is one of the most powerful tools we have. When laughter is shared, it binds people together and increases happiness and intimacy. It strengthens your immune system, boosts your energy, diminishes pain, and protects you from the damaging effects of stress. Best of all, this priceless medicine is fun, free, and easy to use. Watch a funny movie or make someone laugh today through telling a joke or a funny story.

How will you know when you have found your Citrine? By how it makes you feel. Think about some of the happiest people you know in your life and most of them help others. When you find the Citrine it is so powerful that you will never want to let it go...

❀ ❀ ❀

Emerald

Represents: Love

Also represents: Relationships, beauty and style, the natural living world

Day of the Week: Thursday

Colour: Green

Emotion: Love, compassion, kindness, gratitude, intimacy, forgiveness

Affirmations: I alone am responsible for my own happiness
I do not rely on anyone else to make me happy
I love and appreciate myself
When I have learned to love myself, I will be ready to love another fully to know true love — I go within... the answer is within
The world is my family.

Focus on the World: Asia and Eurasia — Celebrate their music, culture, food and wisdom

Quotes: "If you see the soul in every living being — you see truly."
Bhagavad Gita — Hindu holy scripts

"Simplicity, patience, compassion. These three are your greatest treasures."
Lao Tzu — Tao Te Ching — China

❀ ❀ ❀

The Emerald represents Love

Everyone deserves to find love — to love and be loved — but the most important relationship you will ever have is with yourself.

Where is Your Emerald hiding? What does it mean to love yourself? How do we find this love?

We are never taught what self-love is, where it is or how to find it, and yet the journey to find it is the most important journey you will ever make. It is the journey back to your heart — to a space within you, where in the silence and stillness between your thoughts you meet another part of yourself — who you are in your essence — without your fears and worries — pure love...

Self-love encourages you to honour your feelings and needs as a priority; not in a vain and egotistical way, but because when you are happy and fulfilled you will be more effective and able to benefit yourself and those around you. Self-love guides you to take positive actions towards your goals thereby building your self-confidence and self-esteem. Without self-love it can be difficult to move forward and feel a sense of well-being which can then start to impact all areas of our lives.

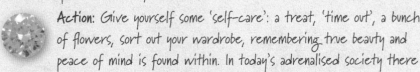

Action: Give yourself some 'self-care': a treat, 'time out', a bunch of flowers, sort out your wardrobe, remembering true beauty and peace of mind is found within. In today's adrenalised society there are huge pressures on many levels, often exacerbated by press and social media which can easily lead to being overloaded and overwhelmed, so meditation and relaxation and self-love are key to balance our lives and give us mental and physical 'time out'.

Our world needs us all to pull together and support the environment. Go for a walk in nature and see the beauty of a wild flower or a magnificent tree, note that they are free just to BE... they have no agenda... no one to impress. They just ARE... let nature teach us. Make a list of everything you are grateful for instead of feeling bad about what you believe you lack.

How will you know when you have found your Emerald? By how it makes you feel when you connect to the peace and love within your heart and this becomes the internal reference point from which you live your life.

Sapphire

Represents: Communication
Also represents: Friendships and social life

Day of the week: Friday

Colour: Blue or turquoise

Emotion: True expression of all emotions, honesty, respect, patience, clarity

Affirmation: I speak my truth clearly
I respect the power of the word and use it with integrity
I remember what peace there is in silence

Focus on the World:
North America, Canada, Arctic circle, Central America and Caribbean — Celebrate their music, culture, food and wisdom

Quotes: "We did not weave the web of life, we are merely a strand in it. Whatever we do to the web we do to ourselves."
Chief Seattle.

"In our every deliberation, we must consider the impact of our decisions on the next seven generations."
Iroquois Confederacy Maxim

❀ ❀ ❀

The Sapphire represents Communication

There are very many ways we communicate with body language, touch, empathy, the tone of our voice, talking and listening skills... silence... Emotional wellbeing stems from the ability to clearly communicate what you want in life. When you have clarity you make good life decisions.

Where is your Sapphire hiding? What clues is it leaving for you... are you communicating with clarity? The meaning of communication is the response you get... If you aren't getting the response you want then you may not be communicating clearly. If you don't know what you want and don't speak up for yourself, or have clear boundaries, you could be in danger of becoming a blank canvas that other stronger characters may colour in... people treat you as you teach them to treat you. Dare to say 'No'... if that is what you mean. Your wants and needs are just as important as anyone else's wants and needs...

Action: Communication also involves listening — Native American Indians used a 'Listening Feather'... only the person holding the feather can speak, after which the listener repeats back exactly what has been said... without judgement... the feather is passed on to the next person... such a great way to tackle a difficult situation as it builds respect and breaks the ice and everyone agrees that it's amazing being listened to without interruption... try it today... with or without a feather!

Also today: We are social beings and love to be seen and heard and feel deeply connected to others to thrive. Spice up your social life and have fun, value your friendships — celebrate your voice, sing in the shower, join a choir, go dancing, write a letter, and if possible try not to judge anyone or anything for at least three hours!

How will you know when you have found your Sapphire? By how it makes you feel when you are able to ask questions and express your thoughts, ideas, emotions and needs with truth and clarity, experiencing a deep sense of wellbeing and joy as you participate fully in life enjoying yourself and the company of others.

❀ ❀ ❀

Lapis Lazuli

Represents: Home environment
Also represents: Family, pets, plants, cooking

Day of the week: Saturday

Colour: Dark Blue — Indigo

Emotion: Intuition, generosity of spirit, hospitality

Affirmation: I see my path ahead with clarity
I follow my intuition

Focus on the World: South America and Antarctica — Celebrate their music, culture, food and wisdom

Quotes: "Song is like the water that washes the stones, the wind that cleanses us, like the fire which joins us together and it lives within us to make us better people."
Victor Jara, Chile

"What matters in life is not what happens to you but what you remember and how you remember it."
Gabriel García Márquez, Colombia

❋ ❋ ❋

The Lapis Lazuli represents Home Environment

Your home is your sanctuary from the rest of the world; your home environment is a reflection of who you are.

Where is your Lapis Lazuli hiding? What clues is it leaving for you? What is your home reflecting about you? Who and what do you have in your life? Do they nourish and sustain you? What can you do to enhance your home environment?

 Actions: Take time to nurture relationships with your family and friends.

Gravitate towards those that naturally create good feelings for you.

Clean and de-clutter your living space and re-cycle your clothes and shoes.

Fill your home with things you love to smell, see, touch and listen to.

Create your own 'chill out' area with your favourite music, books, hobbies and interests.

Nurture your pets and plants and garden.

Experiment with preparing meals from all round the world to share with your family and friends.

How will you know when you have found your Lapis Lazuli?
Because as you start to make even small changes in your environment and start to spend your time with those who make you feel happy, content, relaxed, and surround yourself with what brings you peace and comfort, just watch and see how your life blossoms. It's not selfish to want a happy life — it's your birthright...

❀ ❀ ❀

Amethyst

Represents: Health
Body, Mind and Spirit

Day of the week: Sunday

Colour: Purple

Emotion: Wholeness and balance in all areas of health

Affirmation: I am responsible for my health and well-being —
I acknowledge and appreciate living in the present moment

Focus on the World: Europe — Celebrate their music, culture, food and wisdom

Quotes: "To see a World in a Grain of Sand And a Heaven in a Wild Flower, Hold Infinity in the palm of your hand. And Eternity in an hour."
William Blake, England 1757-1827

"We are not human beings having a spiritual experience. We are spiritual beings having a human experience."
Pierre Teilhard de Chardin, France 1881-1955

The Amethyst represents Health

The word 'health' comes from the Greek word 'holos' or 'holistic' which encourages us to look at ourselves as a whole — Body, Mind and Spirit — and aim for balance in all these areas in order to achieve perfect health.

Where is your Amethyst hiding? What is it leading you to focus on?

Body: Many diseases are caused as a direct result of what we put into our bodies so it makes sense to eat healthily and drink plenty of water — **Action:** Experiment with juicing fresh fruit and vegetables... Exercise releases endorphins which are natural mood enhancers, so start to look at exercise as a treat and aim to be active for at least 40 minutes three or four times a week.

Mind: Every cell in our body reacts to every thought we have. Once we begin to understand the process, we can start to take conscious control of the changes we want to make in our lives. **Action:** Try to choose thoughts that uplift you and question those thoughts that make you unhappy. They are only thoughts and thoughts can be changed.

Spirit: What we have not been taught from a young age is that the internal peace we long for is available to us at any time through the practice of meditation. **Action:** Turn your gaze inwards... correct yourself and your world will change. Aim to practice meditation or simply sit in silence and be still for a least five-ten minutes once or twice a day if you can.

How will you know when you have found your Amethyst? By how it makes you feel when you follow a simple daily routine, thereby effortlessly ensuring you are doing the best you can do for your Body, Mind and Spirit... taking responsibility for your health and well-being will be the best investment you ever make.

❀ ❀ ❀

Diamond

Represents: Balance in all areas of your life

Day of the week: Every day

Colour: Diamond white — reflecting all colours of the rainbow

Emotion: Balance, peace of mind, confidence, courage, trust, respect, bliss, love, intuition

Affirmation: The Diamond within is the internal reference point for my life

Focus on the whole world: Every person, creature and living organism on its surface

Quote: "I wish I could show you when you are lonely or in darkness the astonishing light of your own being"
Hafez 1325–1389

The Diamond represents Balance

As you start to find your jewels and have the courage to move through life's challenges and follow your dreams — you get an incredible prize. A secret compartment opens to reveal a truly magnificent Diamond in your heart — from this Diamond, there emanates an exquisite pure white light reflecting all the colours of each of the jewels, all the colours of the rainbow in perfect harmony. This Diamond light radiates in and around you.

You will understand that everyone has a Diamond in their heart and that everyone is on their own unique journey with different — often difficult lessons — to learn; you will feel compassion for the whole of humanity realising that we are all united in this truth.

You can then take your Diamond light into your life and make a real difference to the future of our world.

The Diamond Greeting

Press your thumb and forefinger together creating the shape of a diamond then place your hand lightly on your heart silently, in your imagination or saying aloud — I salute the Diamond in your heart and my heart...

❀ ❀ ❀

24

Your Rainbow Bridge of Jewels

As you begin your quest to find and polish your unique jewels, the magnificent Diamond in your heart lights up jewelled pathways for you to follow, creating a Rainbow Bridge of Jewels keeping you on track and focused, leading you towards your true destiny.

In order to start your journey of transformation to cross over your Rainbow Bridge of Jewels, spend some time thinking about your dreams and goals for each of the seven jewels — this will help to bring clarity where there may be confusion.

On the following pages you will see your Rainbow Bridge of Jewels 'Dream Sheet' for you to consider and complete in your own time and whenever it feels right for you.

It's important to remember that life is a journey and the landscape is continually changing, which may in turn influence your dreams and aspirations and so you may find that you need to review and update your Dream Sheet from time to time as your life evolves and expands. You can find blank Dreams Sheets on the website.

If it helps, draw your perfect scenario and most importantly believe that your dreams are on their way — how does that make you feel?

It's all about making you feel good, lifting your vibration; we are magnetic beings. We attract in what we believe and focus on. We don't manifest what we want. So get very clear about what you are believing and focusing on in your day and make your focus... your dreams.

"We are such stuff as dreams are made on; and our little life is rounded with a sleep."
The Tempest — Shakespeare

Your Rainbow Bridge of Jewels Dream Sheet

 Ruby – Life purpose, education, work and finances

- What do you want?

- Why do you want it?

- What actions will you take?

 Topaz – Creativity, travel, hobbies

- What do you want?

- Why do you want it?

- What actions will you take?

❀ ❀ ❀

Citrine – Charity – your community, your country, the world

- What do you want?

- Why do you want it?

- What actions will you take?

Emerald – Love, relationships, beauty, style, natural world, the environment

- What do you want?

- Why do you want it?

- What actions will you take?

❀ ❀ ❀   28

Your Rainbow Bridge of Jewels Dream Sheet

 Sapphire – Communication skills, friendships & social life

- What do you want?

- Why do you want it?

- What actions will you take?

 Lapis Lazuli – Home environment, family, pets and work environment

- What do you want?

- Why do you want it?

- What actions will you take?

Amethyst – Health, Body, Mind, Spirit

- What do you want?

- Why do you want it?

- What actions will you take?

 # Diamond – Draw your perfect scenario

PART II

❁ ❁ ❁

Gems of Wisdom

In the following pages are a few 'gems of wisdom' I picked up along the way, as well as some tools I created, which I hope you will find helpful.

There is no such thing as a 'happy happy' life with no sadness and no challenges that is not reality. However, if we can build a relationship with ourselves and gain some understanding about how we work — about how our thoughts and beliefs often 'run the show' — it can make all the difference.

Don't distress yourself with the need to rush or be desperate to solve all your problems immediately. Even though things may not be easy and you may worry about how things will work out — life never stands still — and like a flowing river, change is happening beneath the surface and your current situation is only temporary.

In our essence we are all happy and at peace.

We come into the world as innocent beings — full of pure love and joy with a beautiful diamond shinning from our hearts.

This diamond light reflects all the colours of the rainbow... as though each of its facets were itself a jewel of a different colour.

This diamond light stays with us throughout our lives and never leaves us.

This is who we are in our essence — complete, happy and fulfilled and at peace.

However sadly this is what we have forgotten... and...

This is what we need to remember — awareness is the key.

This place of peace within us — I call it 'The Diamond Field' — lives in the silent spaces between our thoughts.

Even in the midst of the chaos of our lives,

it's like a beacon in The Storm.

We don't need to have money or possessions to access it.

It's available to everyone on the planet,

waiting patiently to welcome us.

It is there in you... now.

❋

The Power of Your Thoughts

Our thoughts, it seems, are everything.

Thoughts create vibrations of energy that, like giant magnets, attract back to you what you give out.

Thoughts create feelings and emotions that we feel and store in our body and make us feel good or bad.

If you think happy thoughts — you will feel... happy.

If you think sad and angry and stressful thoughts — you will feel... sad and angry and stressed.

Repeated thoughts and feelings become beliefs.

Beliefs

Throughout our lives we all have very different experiences — good and bad — which are stored in our sub-conscious as our own set of beliefs.

Many beliefs are collected and stored when we are very young and unable to challenge them, and they end up 'getting stuck' in our subconscious.

These beliefs become the lenses through which we experience the world, creating our day to day reality and affecting how we act and react to everyone and everything. We just presume: "This is just who I am."

Some of the more common false beliefs we may collect are:

"I'm not good enough, I'm not worthy, I'm better than you, I'll never be able to make the changes I need to, I'm not clever enough, I'm alone and I'm not enough, I'm not attractive enough, I'll never find true love, I'll never succeed".

Perhaps you can recognise some of them or think of some others!

Actions: If we aren't clear about our true value, we can quite unknowingly create disempowering cycles of false thoughts and beliefs which take over and cause us to feel pressurised and overwhelmed, leading us to take inappropriate or incomplete action or no action at all, preventing us from achieving our goals. This in turn creates evidence to support our 'I told you so' sad story — thereby keeping these self-perpetuating cycles going.

It's not difficult to see that how this can affect all areas of our lives from relationships, work, and health and financial matters — everything...

These cycles will continue to turn unabated until you have had

❀ ❀ ❀

enough, and with the courage of the tiger, you dare to challenge those false beliefs.

As you change, your focus something starts to shift and you become aware that despite what you're going through or have ever been through — despite this — there is another part of you waiting to burst into a new life and create another story.

When this happens, you start to notice that when you question your stressful thoughts and imagine how you would feel without them, you immediately feel free, calm, and happy and liberated.

You feel as if a weight has been taken off your shoulders.

Life is precious and we all deserve to be happy.

Maybe it's time to put down the heavy bag and lighten your load

Shake out the stone in your shoe

Empty out any false beliefs and sad stories

That feel heavy and are dragging you down

Preventing you from moving forward with ease

Maybe it's time to envision a new life...

Start the treasure hunt to find and polish your unique jewels and

Listen to the messages they have for you

Think new thoughts

Experience new feelings

Create new beliefs

Take new actions

Write another story

A Little Bit About Relationships

The most important relationship you will ever have is with yourself.

As you as you connect more and more to The Diamond Field within through the practice of meditation*, you realise that you have an endless source of peace and strength within you.

As you start to relax and trust in this relationship, allowing it to soothe and comfort you, your trust in life will start to grow.

❀

Without this internal reference point

This Diamond anchor

We are as a tree without roots.....

Swaying in The Storm

We are lost

Totally at the mercy of outside forces

With no anchor

❀

We are often impatient to have a relationship and want it to manifest immediately.

But try to see any waiting time as a gift.

Time to rediscover your jewels and to develop passions that excite you and make you feel purposeful.

Then you will be ready to help and love others in a much more effective way.

❀ ❀ ❀

The 'happily ever after' is about finding the love within yourself rather than looking for someone to fill in the blank gaps.

❀

People treat you as you allow them to treat you.

When you start to know your true worth,

you automatically start to set clear boundaries for your well-being, no longer tolerating people and situations that do not honour you.

You learn not to 'over give' as a way of seeking validation.

You learn to stand up for yourself and speak your truth.

You understand that your wants and needs are just as important as anyone else's wants and needs.

❀

Throughout our lives we collect some beautiful memories and relationships that touch our lives for varying amounts of time, and we never know how things will work out or what other wonderful surprises are waiting for you just around the corner.

Of course, life experiences can be very painful and traumatic leaving us feeling desperate, lonely, angry, confused, hurt, betrayed, and fearful. This is a time to be very gentle with ourselves allowing space and time to heal and soothe our delicate hearts and minds as we go through a proper grieving process.

✳

At times like these, we can find great peace in the practice of meditation where in the silence and the stillness between our thoughts — without our story — we can find rest in The Diamond Field.

*see Part III: Meditation and The Diamond Field

✳

After a while we notice that holding onto past hurt, resentment, regret, fear and shame is preventing us from moving on and feeling happy and whole again, when that is all we really want.

This is when we start to realise that there is a choice to be made:

to carry on feeling as we are or to

change our focus to the future rather than the past.

This is not to say that the hurt never happened,

or diminish its impact on you,

but rather we are no longer allowing it to control our lives.

If we look at our lives as a book — cover to cover — in some chapters we can see where our false beliefs may have led us to behave and act in certain ways.

These insights — once understood — can become the lessons we needed to learn in order to turn ourselves around and get back on track — spurring us on to take responsibility for ourselves and encouraging us,

to write the next incredible chapter.

✳ ✳ ✳

❋

The world needs both feminine and masculine energy to be in balance within individuals as well as externally in the world at large. A world where both male and female energies (which are of course very different in nature, thankfully and beautifully so) celebrate each other and are treated equally.

Throughout history women have been valued for their ability to care and to create balance and harmony. However in this world kindness and compassion have often been seen as weaknesses to be taken advantage of, and there are still many parts of the world where girls and women continue to suffer huge prejudice and injustice.

Thankfully today as more girls and women around the world become educated and start to value themselves, they are finding the confidence to contribute equally to at a time when the world is crying out for what they do best — creating balance and harmony with the ability to care.

We can then all join together, united in mutual respect with a common purpose to spread light not just in our lives, but collectively for the good of our communities, our countries, and the whole planet.

The Two Books of Your Life

Action: Purchase two books or notebooks.

One with an attractive or golden cover and the other with a plain cover.

Start to write your own Books of Life.

Each book is the story of your life.

Each book has been written by you... for you.

The first plain book feels very heavy...

In the plain book write down the top three sad stories that you constantly repeat to yourself and others.

Next write down the top three false beliefs that you have collected about yourself and never questioned and which you drag around with you every day, e.g. 'I'm not good enough' and why you believe your dreams and wishes will never come true.

Note any ways you can see where you may be putting off taking positive actions towards your goals as you don't really believe they will come true. Feel how disempowered and frustrated you feel as, despite all your best efforts, you feel as though you are making no head way in The Storm...

Let me introduce you to The Storm Bugs...

The Storm Bugs

Disempowering Bugs   Bitter Bugs   Royal Bugs

The Storm Bugs live in The Storm of your life and survive on criticism and negativity... these are a few of the characters who might show up in your life...

Disempowering Bugs are disempowered beliefs that you have picked up along the way... They love it when you feel anxious and fearful and say to yourself... I'm not clever enough, I'm not good enough, I'm not worthy, I am not enough... I will never be successful; or whatever your particular sad story is at the time.

Bitter Bugs bear grudges — they don't want you to forgive... they want you to feel bitter, angry, resentful, and jealous as they know that this will keep your heart firmly closed and prevent you from opening your heart to let peace in and allow your life to move forward.

Royal Bugs are like Kings and Queens — very strong characters who seem to have power and influence and no conscience. They press your buttons and send you into a spin and make you doubt your worth. They love to say "I am better than you... you are stupid... you are lucky to know me..."

All Storm Bugs are desperate that you keep feeding them, as that is what keeps them alive and empowered. Some of them look very prosperous...and have done very well on your insecurities and vulnerabilities and have carved out a good life style for themselves... so next time you are feeling sad or triggered, ask yourself, which Storm Bug are you feeding ?!

Good news!

None of The Storm Bugs can survive in The Diamond Field.

The light is too bright.

So when you notice you are paying attention to The Storm Bugs — acknowledge them — and thank them for reminding you that you need to take back control!

The second book is golden. It feels light. It has golden pages with light radiating out of them...

Take some deep breaths to relax — once you feel calm and centered, start to write the story of your life as you would love it to be in all areas, using the messages revealed to you by the Seven Jewels to help and guide you.

It's a story of fulfilment and empowerment where you are taking actions to reflect your true worth.

It's a beautiful story.

Start to listen to the quiet whispering of your Diamond reminding you of who you really are — try to memorise these words if you can.

- I was born completely whole and complete to love and be loved

- I am a unique, wise, wonderful and loving being who has the power and courage to evolve beyond past limiting beliefs

- I have a unique contribution to make in the world

Choices

When you have written both books you will be free to choose which one you want to read.

At any one time — you are reading from one of these books and its story is colouring your reality.

At any one time — you can choose to shut one book and open the other book.

The Five Rings

You can use the five rings as a gauge to see how you are feeling and how close you are to The Diamond Field at the centre.

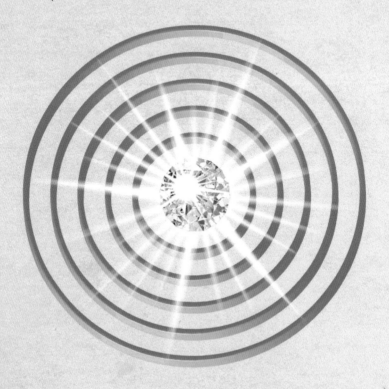

Ring 1   The Inner Ring — The Diamond Field where you are at peace and aligned to your true power.

Ring 2   Feeling good.

Ring 3   Feeling quite good — we often settle here.

Ring 4   Feeling sad and uncomfortable.

Ring 5   The Outer Ring — The Storm where you feel stressed, telling yourself a sad story full of fear, anger and regret.

❀ ❀ ❀

When you find yourself feeling unsettled, acknowledge it and become curious about

- Which ring you are in
- Which book you are reading
- Which Storm Bugs you are feeding.

When you act or re-act from outer Ring 5 — The Storm — your actions and reactions are completely different than if you act and re — act from Ring 1 — The Diamond Field.

Notice also how others react to you depending on which ring you are centered in.

We go in and out of the rings all the time and that's completely normal, so if you find yourself in one of the outer rings don't worry, it could be something as simple as a bad night's sleep, a bad day at work, something someone said or didn't say, to much more difficult situations and issues.

Life never stops happening!

When you are feeling 'shaken up' imagine that you are waiting for stirred up sand to settle in a glass of water — you can't force it — but it will settle eventually.

Above all, be gentle with yourself and use your tools of meditation, SBS and The Diamond Breath to centre yourself back in The Diamond Field (see Part III).

Once you are in the peace of The Diamond Field, you can stay there as long as you like.

From there you can make a better decision about what to do or say and what will be best for yourself and others.

It is where the solution is to be found.

44

Using the Five Rings to make a decision

You can use the Five Rings theory to help you in everyday life to make decisions and to move forward when you 'feel stuck' in The Storm.

When you have a difficult decision to make and you don't know what to do, it's as though you are in Ring 5 — in The Storm — don't make your decision here!

Before making your decision about a person, relationship, work or any situation, start at Ring 5 on the outside and work your way in, ring by ring, getting information and asking relevant questions before you move to the next ring.

As you move towards the centre you will gain more and more information giving you the clarity to make a more informed choice — when we have clarity we can make good life decisions.

Ring 5 Ask relevant questions — get the facts — don't waste time presuming things.

Ring 4 Start to get a sense of how this situation is impacting / would impact you — try not to sugar coat it!

Ring 3 Resting Ring — think over the information and consider your options. Find out where you can get any support you might need and what actions you need to take.

Ring 2 Start to move forward in your own time.

Ring 1 Make your decision — feel your self-esteem rise as you speak and act from the truth of The Diamond Field.

❀ ❀ ❀

Remember what you want and need is just as important as what anyone else wants and needs, so don't feel pressurised to jump into a situation you are not comfortable with; rather say,.

"Let me have a think about it," or, "I'm processing — one ring at a time!"

Remember this is just a guide and you can change your mind at any time.

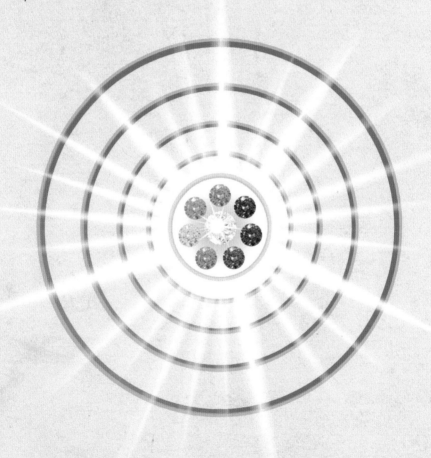

❀ ❀ ❀

PART III

Meditation

What we have not been taught from a young age is that the internal peace we long for is available to us at any time if we want it — we don't have to have money and possessions to get it — it's free to everyone

This oasis is of calm — I call it The Diamond Field - can be found in the silent gap between our thoughts.

We just have to know that this space is there and then understand how to access it — the best way is through the practice of meditation.

If this sounds difficult — it's simply just sitting down and quietening the mind for a few moments.

This silence opens up an inner peace and a natural calm.

All appears as normal on the outside, but within, you are empty, happy and silent.

Instead of trying to change the world to match your thoughts about how you think it should be on the outside — look within.

What do you learn when you slow down and go inside? You find that your focus starts to shift away from your personal story and worries and this gives you a place to rest.

As you practice meditation for as little as five to ten minutes a day, you will develop the confidence to spend more and more time in your own company and begin to notice some amazing changes within yourself.

SBS Technique

In our busy lives we can often be overwhelmed with life's events — rushing around we can feel as if we are making no headway in The Storm.

I am going to share with you a formula so that from now on, when you are feeling stressed and out of balance, you don't dismiss these feelings as though they don't count... take these 3 steps: S. B. S.

S Stop!   Slow down and if possible sit down comfortably and close your eyes

B Breathe   Let go of all thoughts and begin to observe the inflow and outflow of your breath.

Your breath is the key...

Inhale through your nose and exhale slowly and deeply through your mouth or nose.

After a few minutes you will feel yourself calming down.

As your breathing calms, your mind follows... it has no choice...

When you are feeling calm... you will be ready to

S Step   Within... into the peace of the Diamond Field. You can return here whenever you need to — it is always there — a refuge from The Storm.

With practice you will soon get very good at it and then you can join in... the Dance of Life!

❀ ❀ ❀

The Diamond Field

A space of peace and love deep within each one of us

where, without your fears and worries and your personal story,

you meet the Diamond in your heart —

your wise self.

❀

Your Diamond waits patiently to welcome you to your Diamond Field but

it cannot help and guide you unless you ask.

Action:

Go to an area of special significance, either physically or in
your imagination.

Relax and get really comfortable and close your eyes.

Invite your Diamond to join you.

It smiles gently and leads you to share a golden seat,

and listens to your fears and worries with love and compassion
without interruption.

It does not judge or condemn you.

It feels your pain and heartache.

It knows everything you are going through, and everything you have
ever been through.

❀ ❀ ❀

It knows your deepest longings, and what you yearn for.

It will never leave you.

It knows what your unique destiny is.

Its sole purpose is to help and guide a and remind you of your true magnificence.

You ask for guidance... and... wait...

Listen for the answers... to the quiet whisperings of your soul.

"Out beyond the ideas of wrong doing and right doing, there is a field. I'll meet you there." Rumi

❀ ❀ ❀

The Diamond Breath

Find a place where you won't be disturbed.

Sit or stand comfortably and close your eyes.

Let go of all thoughts and begin to observe the inflow and outflow of your breath.

As you continue to breathe in this way, imagine a magnificent Diamond in your heart with diamond light radiating out from it...

On your next breath out see or feel this diamond light flowing all the way down to the base of your spine.

Breathe in.

Breathing out.... see or feel this diamond light go down through your legs.

Breathe in.

Breathing out... see or feel this diamond light coming out of the soles of your feet.

Until it finds a magnificent Diamond in the centre of the earth's core, radiating diamond light... feel yourself anchored firmly here....

Relax here a while... when you are ready,

breathe this diamond light up through your legs and into the base of your spine...

Breathe out to relax.

Breathe the diamond light up through the centre of your body to connect with a magnificent Diamond in your heart... breathe out to relax.

Breathe the diamond light up from your heart to the crown of your head... breathe out to relax.

Now... see or feel this river of diamond light flowing out of your head to connect to a magnificent diamond star high above you. From this star there emanates a pure white light reflecting all the colours of the rainbow in perfect harmony.

Breathe out to relax.

You now have a channel between the Diamond at the centre of the earth, the Diamond in your heart and the Diamond star high above in the universe...

See or feel this diamond light like a river of joy flowing up and down this channel — every time you breathe in and out, radiating love and peace to you and every cell in your mind and body... you may feel tingling in your body... this is the Diamond's gift to you... rest here as long as you want to in The Diamond Field.

Finally put your attention on the Diamond in your heart... feel your heart opening and bathing in the diamond light... place both your hands on your heart and on your next breath out, push both hands out in a circle around you as though you were pushing this diamond light all around you... all around the world.

On your next breath in — bring your arms back to the centre — resting your hands on your heart — bringing the light back to yourself.

Rest here a while...

When you feel ready and in your own time — gently open your eyes and take a few moments to savour the peace of the diamond light.

Daily Routine – Your Diamond Day

Creating a simple and enjoyable daily routine keeps us on track, centered... focused and happy... after a while it will become second nature... The Diamond Day incorporates an aspect of each jewel within it. We all lead such different lives — and this is just one suggestion...

Create a 'special area' in a corner of a room where you could place a candle, some flowers and some items of significance to you.

On waking — stretch... and greet the day... smile and say to yourself... I welcome and look forward to this new day and to taking responsibility for my own happiness and actions — not relying on anyone else to sing my song for me...

Spend a few moments doing some gentle exercise or yoga and meditation.

Drink a glass of water or make a cup of tea then go to your 'special area' sit down and relax as you enjoy the next few moments of quiet reflection.

Open up your Seven Jewels of Life Book and read the Jewel of the day.

• In a small book — make a note of what you need to do to feel organised for the day ahead and plan the actions to take towards your dreams and goals

Get dressed and ready for the day... enjoy this time take a pride in how you look — you could choose something to wear that reflects the colour of the Jewel of the Day...

Breakfast: Enjoy a healthy breakfast.

On your way to work if you can listen to an inspirational tape or read a good book.

A box of treasures to use throughout the day:-

• At work, be focused and creative

• Do some form of exercise

• Eat healthily and drink plenty of water

• Meditate for five minutes whenever you can

• SBS when you feel stressed to centre yourself

• Memorise a positive truth statement to say to yourself

• Look at your Dream Sheet — to lift you and keep you on track

 At the end of the day, light a candle to welcome in the evening. Relax and listen to some soothing music... close your eyes and think about people, situations in your life and in the world that you would like to send love to.

You could share food from the continent of the day with family and friends.

Relax and enjoy this last part of the day...

Before you go to sleep remember all the things in your life to be grateful for and affirm that you will sleep deeply and soundly, waking in the morning bright and refreshed and looking forward to a new Diamond Day ahead.

❀ ❀ ❀

Revelations and Thoughts written at The Tree of Life in Auroville, Pondicherry, India 2013 by Belinda Jane Robinson

There is a Tree in India

With branches to the sky

I climbed up to the top of it

And stood upon a Star

The world was far below me now

A green and turquoise ball

The view was awe-inspiring

My mind was calm and clear

Roots went down to liquid gold

And found a Diamond anchor

It pulsated love and light to all

And Silence was its mantra

Diamond light flowed through my veins

And settled in my Heart

It soothed my Soul

And made me whole

And sweetly gave the answer

It was as if

Time stood still

It was a precious moment

It whispered that

We all should know

The Diamond at our Centre.

❀ ❀ ❀

Glossary

The Diamond Field: A place in the heart of you where you can find rest from The Storm of life... a place of peace and love that lives in the gap between your thoughts... it is where your Diamond – your Wise Self lives... the best way to access this place is through the practice of Meditation... S B S... The Diamond Breath.

The Wise Self: The part of you that lies within – the Diamond in your heart – the you without your worries and personal story – who is strong and complete – free from pain and fear.

The Storm: The part of life where you feel out of control – sad and disempowered – where you have no anchor and feel that life is happening to you not through you – where you feel like the victim and helpless.

The Diamond Breath: A powerful meditation and breathing technique which aligns you to three diamonds – one at the centre of the earth – one in your heart and one above you.

Serpentine Stone: Originally this altered peridotite was thought to be the root of a volcano, but it is now recognised to be part of the earth's mantle. It is a beautiful green and red stone veined with white and in the United Kingdom is only found on the Lizard peninsular, in Cornwall. The lighter green stone is valued for its meditative properties.

Gully-Gully men: Traders who trade their wares in the Suez Canal.

Printed in Great Britain
by Amazon

37435964R00039